MW00627479

On the *Cusp*
of Memory

On the *Cusp* of Memory

RANDY PRUS

ILLUSTRATIONS BY ETHAN PRUS

On the Cusp of Memory
Copyright ©2015 Randy Prus

ISBN: 978-1-940769-42-4
Publisher: Mercury HeartLink
Printed in the United States of America

Illustrations by Ethan Prus, *jelloween.com*

Contact the author at: *randyprus@gmail.com*

Mercury HeartLink
www.heartlink.com

Contents

Introduction

It's not the wanting, but the giving. Take what you need, leave the rest, pass these moments along.

These poems were written with a sense of gratitude and generosity. They are only what I found and further on to the reader. I've compressed, and at times expanded, the examinations into fourteen lines. Call them sonnets or call them what you will. They are a call out from someplace called southern Oklahoma, from some time marked as the early 21st century, a brief moment in the Anthropocene epoch. If I lend too much to time and space, it's because they inhabit the poems as much as I do, many times over. Love leaves laughter. My son, Ethan, has grown. His art echoes this work, and fills my silence. It is past midnight as I write this, on a Thursday on a cool night in a year I can't identify.

If read accordingly, along with the illustrations, one might find different spaces, different time frames as well as registers, and different projections of the self, each as the occasion necessitated itself. Plus, I had a lot of fun writing them.

But I am Sirius. And, here, I do call your attention to the cover illustration by my son as well as to the illustration to the poem, "I am Sirius." He is an artist in ways much different than I am. Where words are my difficulty, ink and pen electronically are his. He is the better craftsman. My advantage is that we grew up together, and my son is the father of the man. The days of the past are upon us, and history rests upon the memory of history. Memory and History are dialectically opposed, thus the title of this work: *On the Cusp of Memory*. The work, here, is neither history nor memory, but poetry and illustration, containing both history and memory. This is the peace I sleep with. My son's hours are not my own. All of this should sound familiar—and it is—while, hopefully appearing strange. I see Art as the intermingling of the strange with the familiar. We come across our lives in mysterious ways. Ethan and I did.

Randy Prus
September 2015
Durant, Oklahoma

for
Nanny & Pops

On the Cusp
of Memory

we are always living
by the sea, salt-foam & spray,
no matter how inland it gets

eighty some million years ago,
relatively a stone's skip
Oklahoma was shoreline

this place, where I now live
was once beachfront property
before property became important

the crustaceans became
limestone deposits forming
hills as the sandstone eroded

the sea is always underfoot,
the one life we have

Geo-logos

1

death circles us like a puppy
on a long walk, exercising
the most important urgencies

the body is a language
perhaps more dear since
we don't have a language

of death, we are certain
of certain things, the ribald
meeting of stars & constellations

but how we connect the dots
in the night performs
the path of our doing

we got in this together,
& we will get out alone

Can I do you?

the east of this country
with its genocidal tendencies
sees place as "property"

yet kept the names: Parsipanny,
Weehawkin, Piscataway,
as a tribute to conquest

the west of this country
with its containment policy
sees place as "land"

a wide expanse of possibility
as long as the fences are mended
unless need be otherwise

some stories unfold,
others are never told

The Acre as Poetic Measure

the trick is, is to get back
to that place of unfolding
before it becomes a crease

the movement along narrative
lines had to be different,
how else to understand

the difference, lines become
broken, out of necessity,
we can not tell it, otherwise

speak it, unless the measure
disrupts accordingly an
understanding of the song

it has all been said, we,
the people, just can't write it

What happened to the pen?

7

after paychecks, all we have
to come home to, is the books,
cook them how we may

our telling is an accuracy
along different lines,
a profit not yet awarded

this is the difficulty of commerce
& of poetry, our ledgers invite
no common bottom lines

we have off-shore investments,
people who invest in us never
realize, and never know

but isn't this the only system
this country has ever known

Poetry as Free Enterprise

the vector force of matter
impinges upon us in ways
not quite legible

each image or sound a blow,
a force of substance from a nature
of which we aren't prepared

each word a blow, from us,
onto that world, that outside,
which we lost, sometime back:

rage, anxiety, comfort, lust,
the search for answers unfilled,
shape ourselves to what we are

human, searching for a place,
searching for a narrative

Writing as a Search for Difficulty

that words come inside
sometimes is a matter
of seasons, winter

how the moon tonight
will last longer than
other moons, we know

it isn't the cold this time
of year, but our bookish
pretentiousness, when else

to spend long hours reading
than when the earth is quiet,
ourselves, full of the harvest,

long texts extend the light,
even when the light is silent

A Long Moon & a Shortened Sky

as if people were writing
as writing were a people
Jefferson wrote out

"all men are created equal"
with certain inalienable rights
"...and the pursuit of happiness"

poets have read this text
as Homeric in function
some creed in which Jefferson

tells us how to steer the ship
of state, but too many of us
have become Jacksonian

asking for the spoils, when
the spoils have become us

An Independence to Obedience

take Polk, for instance,
wanting land for pure land,
& calling it territory

arguing the threat, the other,
the Mexicans, & the silent
Whig voice in Congress

& the voice of the press
of hey "they" need civilization
more sooner, because....

the press wrote "Manifest
Destiny" so large in the history
books of my childhood

we need to investigate
the Polk administration

How to think about foreign policy

who else, but us, could become
us, we've had the word, the *logos*
from the beginning

and the beginning said "all
men" and "we the people"
and then later "for" and "of"

the same people we fought
"for" and "of" off again
for many years after,

it's the "after" which plagues
us into thinking the war
is always already over

we write new beginnings
over old texts

When reading isn't enough

I first saw her in the autumn
on a street corner, just off
Tremont in Boston

she was silent, but her
story was the dark-haired
legend, I'd been looking for

her, a thousand nights,
in the books & dust
of libraries & taverns

she wasn't love, but she
created it, the tough kind
that leaves one lonely

she didn't see me & then
she looked the other way

November 1975

heaven is the emptiness
stolen by thought, or all
that which evades history

& the touch of the green leaf
in springtime as it is re-membered,
put back as it were, silent twigs

in the silent hours, of the long moon,
in December, when each line is
stretched, absorbing the emptiness

heaven is the repetition
of the already known,
a silence between the tactile

touching you touches me,
how sad to think otherwise

Alone on a Park Bench

all our giving is a forgetting,
whether it be love or landscapes
the movement is gentle

we can only paint that
which we never knew,
but in painting, know it

the aura is that which knows
the knower's knowing, the rise
in the field of eroding sandstone

the limestone's resistance
to wind and water, the lovers'
resistance to each other

this is how form begins,
this is how love is

Mondrian in Southern Oklahoma

knowing is the condensing
of all that is "other"
into one's self, a stance

of absorption and projection
the world uttered or muttered
as language will allow

the word & the world
never truly touch, yet
the distance brings love,

the sublime sense of belonging
to others who will not hear you,
of others we cannot touch,

we cannot do, what can't be done,
we can only say, what can't be said

Mr. Kant meet Jesus Christ

we've gotten lost in ourselves
the trick is to find the outside
again as language

the pear tree in the front yard
blooms once a year, and so
the word can't bear fruit

except on occasions
of its own loveliness
at certain times of the year

between water & sunlight
the word, the fruit, nurtures us
finding us in a certain place

in the richness of the soil,
in etymologies long displaced

The Word in the Garden

war, ultimately, is an administrative
function, used by those who attempt
to understand the exterior of the word

by bringing the utterance,
or otherness, to a performative
masking as a declarative

Polk knew this intuitively
and did so from the Executive
position, one given

to words as a performative,
war is the continuation
of politics, by other means

but it is the work of poets,
and should remain so

Commander-in-Chief

the days linger upon us,
we return to our books
we continue with meaning,

the bottom-line, thought
as if anything could or should
replace it, the stuff of dreams

nights linger when we talk
to the dead, ourselves, in bed
& expect them to walk us

through landscapes, through
places they've imagined
& settle down to tea

to tell us in dreams
they are still living

They do?

if the past is prologue,
prologue to what? I have
a puppy, he came to me

in the fall of the year,
I feed him & pat his head,
he is childhood, to me

I seldom go there, he does,
never to return, he likes
to lick my hand, thoughtfully

he responds to me as if I
were the cold night sky,
Sirius, about him

he wags his tail,
a tale to be remembered

I had it once, then lost it,
thankfully

the conduits
of the sacred heart
lead eventually

to the front door
at which some jesus
monger appears selling

the easy approach
to salvation through
both church or flag

their motto is simple
"believe in me" & let men
die on the cross

but at your door,
clutch your wallets

Hemorrhaging

the voices you heard
is now the voice within
brother where art thou

my blue eyed son
blowin' in the wind
we won't be fooled again

to walk on the wild side
or to love the one you're with
and can't get no satisfaction

somewhere in Winslow, Arizona
behind blue eyes, hoping
to die before one gets old

down ancient empty streets
& a discarded radio

Echoes of My Youth

what did Walt know
when he lay dying?
this is important

as the 1892 edition
of his leaves & leaving
is the "deathbed" one

did he realize he couldn't
compile one life or one
nation out of the many?

the winds of empire
scattered the multiple events
that brought him here

did he know in a democracy,
hegemony isn't possible?

Three Questions

if poetry is a *mappe munde*
how then to chart the rivers
running through it?

freed from its banks, flood-tide,
marks a desire of its own crossing,
an excess & an absence

each crossing enters us
into the ancient newness
of old beginnings

in order to be claimed
the world must be mapped
tracing the flow of rivers

the poem is the continual
excess & absence of words

Mappe Munde

a pecan, like a thought,
simply fell at my feet today
with a tough outer shell

the sun was falling, the sky
was changing from twilight
to Sirius overhead

the dog picked at its outer shell
& played with it awhile
but he, too, couldn't crack it

looking up, the tree was full,
with nuts that would later arrive
scattering its own democracy

but there are not enough dogs
& not enough me to make a pie

I'm Sirius

Oh, Walt how we failed, you
didn't know this world or yours
but you made them possible

you understood people
who make the common
possible, what we are

like the fireman entering
a burning building to save
lives, only to lose his

in your lower Manhattan
lives were lost saving
the lives that were lost

Walt, we need a wound-dresser,
to kiss the lips of a dying nation

With Breastbone Broken

this cold crust of ground, still
forming, we've become part
of its shifts and changes

as if reaching into the past
reached into the fact or reason
the January moon unsettles

it is cold, here, where I live,
I choose it that way, I see
things better in this light

tonight, the dog crept along
in shadows of the house, while
moonlight eclipsed Sirius overhead

the dog & I both know we've
been here a very long time

Sirius January/Serious Cold

after everything, the something,
the beyond after the writing,
the something like January

or metaphor as a sky
of changing horizons
only felt or heard at dusk

for years, starlings gathered
in the morning flying west,
& then in evening flew east,

their flight became a clock
incrementing the sky,
the ground I stood upon

this time, either they or I
have changed course

Where have all the starlings gone...
long time ago

how did we get here?
to this, a cold Wednesday
afternoon in late Pleistocene

embedded in rock & narrative,
the story is incomplete, only
to be re-invented from the pieces

we scratch surfaces, searching
for both subject & subjectivity
only to find our own

this morning, the dog's dish
held a thin layer of ice, so cold
& almost perfect in its shape

but it broke apart as I tried
to make it a symbol

   Ice

this country grows on one,
like a cyst, its rhetoric
gets under the skin, until

the skin is all one sees,
the many has become one,
at the expense of the many,

for the one has the money
to make honey around
the hive, surrounding

the Capital & local towns
the rooks are circling tonight
as if nature knew the game

in descending swallows,
they know what I do

Check

how the mouth figures
the other, in words
and kisses, the separation

allows the impulse
to speak or fuck
to simply happen

as if going about
the everyday world
& we in it was an accident

of cosmic design, we,
that is us, can never
know otherness

which is why we try,
over and over again

A Poem for You

since knowledge is power
over the other, we become
confused stargazers

sentimental to the point
of reducing emotion
to Hallmark cards

our love is conventional,
in order to exist in the world,
we convene our emotions

unless its politics, then
any emotion goes
save dumb reason

we have made this world
& now we have to live in it

Save Dumb Reason

liberalism gave us
the citizen, possessor
of public & private spheres

for two centuries we relied
on this principle from Madison
through the New Deal

but the National Security Act
made the public & the public's
trust a private affair

& Clinton's blowjob so turned
the private into a national
spectacle for the "liberal" media

we have crossed rivers,
the Potomac our Rubicon

Clinton's Blowjob

we are so uncertain
in our formalities, we
say "hello" to anyone

as if the grace of our
blessing extended
past our knowing

but we are Americans
we sell ourselves,
cheaply & often,

we should keep this
in mind: the product
of desire is desire

as a "happy" people,
we pursue happiness

The Declaration as Slogan

the late winter
has caught up with us
almost without surprise

we move through seasons,
as if they were years,
as if they were epochs

& then suddenly, almost,
something has vanished,
beyond the beyond

Henry Adams named this
"education" & held the loss
as history, his & ours

yet this winter is different
almost forgetting its spring

Elegy to the Republic

(After Motherwell)

there is something
that doesn't like Robert Frost
but somehow likes the wall

a harsh New Englander
he gave New Hampshire
what it deserves: a granite will

& a tendency to drift off
its sixteen miles of coastline
into the Atlantic, a terrible

beauty engulfs the place,
cold & hard, Emerson's
frontier of Boston

building walls invites
a neighbor, even Frost knew that

Note: discard, not right

a boy's will is not his own,
with no sense of the sublime,
each event is his own doing

unlike the man witnessing
a late season storm, who
sees abstraction in whiteness

the wind & the snow
the cold on the skin
become, for the man, a force

measured against others:
his life a sum of forces,
neither nature nor memory

but the boy, sees the snow,
& declares a "snow day"

New England snow in southern
Oklahoma

life as vector forces
displaces the human
onto the map of writing

forgetting all along
the body is a map
written large, a *mappe munde*

neither history nor memory,
not nature or a forgetting,
not love or its trace

the last thing known
is the first touch,
begun again anew

desire, the paper on which
we write ourselves

A return to new maps

when all else drips
to liquid &, our substance
has changed, we can

not hold history
in cold palms as
if it were a snowball

to be flung mercilessly
in some other direction
than against our flesh

despite our pieties,
the world isn't a "something"
we can control, or need to

history is an eternal fire
we, the people, don't understand

Except maybe Henry Adams

the jonquils bloomed
suddenly in their late
winter excitement

hoping to turn a new leaf
on the south side of the house
in an old flower bed

then with equal suddenness
the were submerged
beneath the whiteness

of a late season storm
lasting too long to be
anything but beauty

like love, flowers & storm
are best when sudden

Love as Suddenness

the movement from here
to there just might be
elsewhere, a map uncertain

as a poem may be disturbed
by coincidences beyond
what one person can do

like an irritating phone call,
a knock at a door, a war,
or a sudden call to violence

poetry doesn't sit back,
to marvel at creation,
but intervenes into creation

its movement isn't from here
to there, but to elsewhere

A Furthering of the Map

on the steps to a building
we discuss origins
& movements of people

across the wide terrain
of earth without a suitable
map to situate ourselves

and then move inside
the architecture of history,
absorbed by it, complacent

in our knowing, knowing
what we know recognizes
only our own knowing

disturbed by difference,
history is written on the skin

A Poem for Bill Fridley

whose history have we, the people,
become? a terrain blanketed
in cold rain & mist

Lee didn't gain from Antietam
although McClellan botched
the chance to finish

the old gray bastard, just
as John Brown blew his chance
to liberate the Shenandoah

just as we attempt to liberate
others according to the act
and conventions of war

& still we confuse liberty
with killing, war with peace

War, an Old Gray Bastard

if history is chance, why are
armed militia patrolling Newark
airport in March of 2003,

where an American flag costs
$4.95 at the concession booth?
too expensive I tell my son

who seems as confused as I am
wondering what the war
& an airplane ride will bring

lifting off we search for absent
towers, signifying a history
beyond our control, knowing

we will arrive eventually
in a much later world

The Market of History

in love, twilight sings
along the branches,
budding oaks & sweet gum

it is difficult to distinguish
between the two, love
or budding, budding or love

still, we return to the pages
incapable of the history
returning the flower or bird

awakening each morning.
we find ourselves, without
our own histories only

with love and a bud,
some new kind of morning

Spring is Here

this morning, the radio played
"Radio-Free Shreveport," an aftermath
of Daylight Savings Time

celebrating "patriot" rallies
in Bossier, along the slave delta
in the year 2003, while US troops

entered Baghdad, not Vicksburg
as they did in 1863, the day
after Lee fucked up Gettysburg

history is marked by battles,
some too recent to mention,
Antietam & Tet, to name two

half the nation lost a war, once,
refusing to remember

Our Wars, Our History

of love, and history, the two
almost forms the self,
disruptive, yet there

yet the not-yet moments
of one's life reflects angularly
in the life of one's day

love appears while one
happens to, or not, while
doing dishes or taking out

the trash, suddenly something
appears, last week's news,
or the chance to buy difference

historians will read the papers
we use differently

History as News

and when Emily read
the news, deciding life
was indeed a "loaded gun"

she knew better to "load
up" in her chamber,
writing more about chamber

pots, and their usefulness
as far as poetry is concerned
as suddenly as the spider

creeping across her ass
in the wee hours of the morning,
as soldiers died, far from her,

as they died, she wrote her
strange poems of a nation

Poem for Jeanne Holland

words are hardly transparent
nor can a word be inerrant,
so how can people think?

no wonder there is a war on
both here, and on TV, a people
imposing words on others

in this great land, of "ours,"
words become images, subtlety
becoming the truth of "us"

Jefferson's great wall of separation
was to keep others in the garden,
tending to the fields & empire

no wonder we're all Baptists,
when we need, or want to be

A Poem for an Ex-Preacher

why strike at the moon
when you can bring laughter
into this world, all thought

is only a joke among ourselves,
we have tried precision,
but that has lasted only so long

the gods of our choice aren't
the gods of out fate yet we outlast
them in the end, the night

is rich in metaphors of our own
doing, but doing happens to us
our sorrows can't be healed

by word or symbols, the way
moonlight begins a pavement

Poem for Cliff Marks

the contingencies of love,
how we travel, lies waiting
whether in airport lobbies

or in the wide-expanse
of a car moving along
a plane arcing toward a horizon

the ends of a straight line
diminish in space, we talk,
we grow older, we talk some more

as if the movement of memory
were the path to a destination,
the someplace else we discover

with tired feet, we prove old things
old, new things new, or not so

Upon Returning

ourselves, a result of the outside,
not as distance from the world,
measurable, but the world itself

we have not come much further
than how we started, speech,
the direct action of inscription,

we talk as we imagine ourselves
to be, and in being become that
which we so imagine, ourselves

the measured distance between
this world and that one, the word
a tool, an instrument, recording

the facts of ourselves, so clear
& yet so distant from what we are

After Maximus

work is not so much pain,
but the punishment of memory
& so we abide ourselves

in the luxury of doing that
which has so little bearing
on the consequence of our being

each day begins with a coffee-insistence
on production as if it were words
spilling over from a sentence

& each night ends in a sleepless
slumber of an excess of words
and their meanings, dreams

we begin with so little
yet end with so much

Poem for John Mischo

in another age, *innocence*,
was used ironically, until
power became ourselves

without our knowing,
still living in the despair
of being a victim, first

by England, thanks to
Jefferson & Paine, second
to those who contained us

revolution is what sustained us,
first in might, then in thought,
we are, after all, Romantic

history has taught us nothing,
except to move beyond borders

Revolution as a Tomb

compared to Berlioz, for example,
Douglass traces the transformation
from feudalism through his body

coming across state lines, he
exposed the darkness of the psyche
holding everything in its place

he fled the garden & the garden
as an idea of a "good place"
& fled a world without reason

as an *invisible agency* he wrote
large, large enough for us to see,
a man, more principled than

principle, more of a man,
than even principle allows

An Homage to Frederick Douglass,
because I like him.

as dust, we don't know
what dust we will return to,
the dark earth of the prairie,

the red clay of Georgia,
some sweet river bottom
along a coastline, changing,

some incredibly sweet
mountain top calcified
with the bones of lovers

where else can we reside
except as part of *this*, some
formation of earth we know,

and love, and love to get
at the bottom of *it*

And from Dust You Will Remain

because I'm in love with Amy
sings Mel Torme, and because
everyone is in love with Amy

the jazz scat becomes
the velvet fog of our language
whether walking down the street

or sitting alone on a velvet
cushion in a lonely room,
our voices become one voice

this sadness reaches me, in my
indirect tiredness of trying,
of having to try at love

because I'm in love with Amy,
everyone is in live with Amy

The Velvet Fog

our lives are nothing,
but the work and dreams
we cause them to be

the poems we read,
the music we listen to,
the art we imagine, all

steadfast objects in a place
where steadfast objects abound,
whether a room or a sentence

love is like this, we place
two things between each other,
the word we speak, the one

we eventually tell to the other,
listening with their own words

Time to Move On

origins are the problem,
the movement "from" implies
an "elsewhere," an otherness

from which we are, like love,
yet unlike love, we are not
the toys of accumulation

as if two lovers could speak
the gnarled language of reflection,
of having to be, and to be one

in this world, love has its other
doings, like two people hugging
in crowded confines, never finishing

to say what is important yet leaving
to find the words that do so

In Song or in Words

may's full moon, articulating
desire, arcs across the tree
swollen sky, remembering

only its last moon & desire,
when April trees walked
so close to love, or something

like the vernal darkness
freshly spent by the spell of rain,
or the memory of having walked

here before, the scent of love's
clouded darkness, what has love
become in spring's darkness,

occluded skies asking only
the possible may be possible

How I love the Green Pear Tree

115

in wanting to write, to write
about love, one is misled,
the June rains come suddenly,

their downpours, torrential,
their effect a thickening
of the green around us

oaks become thicker, the once
dry, fragile pecan, grows back,
becoming once more, stately

love is about trees, yes,
but also about coffee cups
collected in a sink, unwashed,

thick branches burden us,
in an afternoon of activity

Clearing away the Domestic, for
Mike.

much like Hamlet, the condition
of the country has come to our being,
we can't escape our own ghosts,

and settle where we are to be,
or not to be, language dawns
upon us, at intimate moments

I do escape the dew of love,
walking across eastern hill,
in mourning clad light

and yet somehow return
to the dust and the dirt
of mine own beginnings

each word, a fleck, ourselves,
an understanding, a moment....

For Glenda, and her father.

the evening so settles us,
like a fifth act, in *Hamlet*,
where we finally understand

divinity and man to be
the same circuitous route
of words, words, words,

and how those words
give us such formations
as the question, "who's there?"

& who is there for us, this
evening, among the quiet
questions words unfold,

we are only as we seem to be,
with words, the night's sky

Hamlet, as Van Gogh

for all these memories,
a remuneration of the body
the morning will unfold,

& we will never get right,
the syntax of dying,
& the syntax dying unfolds,

unlike the leaf, the flower,
we move, linguistically,
backward toward the seed,

& in finding many origins,
find the one origin, the one
word, we call, simply, "father"

eventually we trace his death,
towards us, towards others

Re-membering

the problem with love:
we bring ourselves into
something, a world, we

can and can never know,
as if the seed from the tree
resembles its own distance,

an electron from an atom,
a star from some position,
in a distant galaxy, a child

from the parent loving him,
we come to these investigations
both tired and withdrawn,

my love is morning against
the skin & trying to tell you this

An Allegory of Love

all day long a headache
about thinking of fathers,
& what fathers might be

did Jefferson actually love
his concubine, Hamilton
a libertine, Aaron Burr

at least one story goes,
shot the one accusing
him of his daughter's incest,

a winter's tale to be exact,
& what did Martha feel,
feeling George's wooden teeth

what one does to a woman,
one does becoming a country

The Founding Fathers

all day long, thinking about
the scat song of Amy,
"everyone is in love with Amy"

& then seeing the vortex,
of song & love & flower
walking along a magnolia

in the deep recesses of love,
and a campus, designed
for thinking in other ways,

of how we never allowed
ourselves to get here, a pure
happiness of being, of love

the intellect has become us,
only a moment of passing

A Fleck, Passing

between life & death, one
wanders down streets, too hot
for day, too cold for night

at times, as if one knows
where one is going, or
from where one came,

having only a dictionary
& a pocket of philosophy,
unopened or misused

& every cent is spent
making the perfect unknown,
scraping soles on concrete

measuring the years & miles
our lives have come

The One, and the Many

how often do we succumb
to some understanding
of ourselves, each other

except through small readings,
or the breadth of the view
from our front porch

we take possession from
what we know or see
yet extend that globally

I prefer the crowded
comfort of my own
confusions, distributed

locally, making the world
smaller but larger, by degree

Poem for Kim McGehee

ourselves, scattered
to haymaking, summer
finds ourselves in daylight

yet short on time, the past
year a recollection of such,
the passing, a reminder

of the work, still needed
to do, the work of living,
of loving, the difficulties

abound, small things grow
in my hand, smaller events
take on a significance

the pear tree, planted two
years ago, is bearing fruit

Summer Daze

you're still small, though
your body has grown, your
mind has expanded mine

rich in deposits, we,
together, explore, excavate
a richness that has settled

among us, until the earth,
beneath our feet feels almost
welcomed to become home

sweet love enriches us,
we become as we love,
& love is necessary, sweet

purple flowers at our door,
both leaving & coming home

Poem for Ethan

why does every event become
a problem? problematic
as the discourse goes

can we actually transcend
ourselves to see a larger picture?
I saw some photographs

the other day, of other days,
in them I didn't look capable
of understanding a world

in them I'm young or drunk,
or deeply confused, much
like it is today, with or

without us, a narrative collects us,
more an image than subjectivity

Don't You See!!!!

the fact of love
is ordinarily a whisper,
or, perhaps, an echo

a trying rhythm, what
we've learned and yet
never quite experienced

seldom does the ordinary
amount to such, but it does
& so *dolce* & *doceat* merge

on an ordinary day, too
ordinal to count, some one
brings us a love so changing,

we recognize it, at once,
again, for the first time

Poem for Karen

I have missed me missing
you, today, we celebrate
our independence, separately

& go about our lives, knowing
the meaning of a firecracker,
or the burst of flower against

the star-lit sky, or knowing
how the moon can be blue
in the afternoon, or how

the sun awaits your presence
upon the dew, walking away
from me, but actually towards

the something we have is
the always, already, each day

Independence Day

where do we find ourselves?
in our experience, in both
our time and temperament

& I find myself reading, again,
the texts which brought me here,
by the slow road, one most taken

arriving late, I have found love
to be the best of circumstances,
a condition just past the one

I'm in, love, is like that, always,
putting a comma between
a preposition and its object

gnarling the grammar the world
expects, of us otherwise

Because You're Not Here

for all these thoughts, history
doesn't quite find us here
today, the "Declaration"

a celebration of discarded
fireworks in the gutter, wrappers
torn with no content, except

to say the boys have moved
on, toward other boy things,
a pretense of war in a world

torn up, and left in piles, where
someone is building a parking
lot, while others watch in dismay

it is July 6th, still we find nothing,
nothing resembling an idea

Weapons of Mass Destruction

all through the night, the boys
fought with glorious pride,
trying at the end of punks,

to light victorious fireworks,
M-100s, firecrackers, something
else to light the night sky,

so rich in firmament, delusions
are necessary to bring us here,
so much a nation, so divided,

as if spectral evidence is necessary,
as if the ramparts we bear, as if
we gave a shit about the difference

until men play boyish games, lighting
their spectacle of mass destruction

Fireworks on the Lawn

an afternoon with you
would be sufficient
to discuss our ordinariness

but there is so much more
a lifetime of evenings can't
begin to embrace, how

honeysuckle lingers
on the sunset, the ripeness
of pears hanging on a branch,

or the way the dog's head
tilts askew as I sing you,
an urgency too big to hold,

shadows in moonlight,
when I whisper your name

An Urgency

heroism is reserved for gods
& generals & so we never
see them here, but on screen

life is smaller than that, but
still the repetition of war
makes someone look good,

& if not good, better than
the patriotic gore, the shorter
wars fail to teach us

people die, lives & life
become confused & confusing,
searching channels, we eventually

stumble upon bad reception:
I want to hold your hand

Of Gods, Generals & the History
Channel

where do you go to,
when you're not here?
to some lavender creek perhaps?

or to those tiny spaces between
the thinking & the thought?
I would follow you there, I can't

help myself, the summer has
grown tired of its own mischief,
the grasses have already browned,

the dog star yelps in the sky,
as I walk the dog on sultry
solitary evenings, remembering you,

only in my life does a dying world
signify something like hope

Lavender Creek

where can we go from here?
Gaugin asked a similar question
& painted, the purples & yellows

he knew about love, this comes
in his work, the purples & yellows
a love, the earth tones another

mood, less somnambulant than
the figures guarding the art,
Gaugin arrived at the someplace

else, differently so, as we could,
the crepe myrtles, late with color,
guard our own abstractions, we

cross our own boundaries, living,
& loving them as we must

Gaugin, in Southern Oklahoma

and then again, once the question
is asked, the inquiry has always
already begun, just ask any

district attorney, or counselor,
or nosey neighbor, anyone
who has any interest in our affairs

as with love, we assume questions
will arrive at our doorstep,
like mis-sent mail, annoying

but proof we do have lives
others are trying to expose,
my mailbox warms in July light,

but our questions are ours,
guarded by the voices we bring

Where do we go from here?

falling in love with love
is like falling into an evening
chair, falling for you

comes more comfortably,
we can discuss lyrical
boundaries, our songs

& the songs of Lorenz Hart,
who brings my heart a-glitter
on black & white film,

how else can one fall
into love, but by listening:
the music of the night

hums, in my movements,
quieting the house to sleep

We Are Here

it is hot here, as I'm sure
where you are too, summer
lingers like a blister on the skin

I have never felt this way,
before or after, & finally
I like the place I live

history no longer touches me
here, the world is a long
ways off, somewhere, over there

beyond an overcrowded shelf,
where you aren't, but I would
be there, to place you here,

as you sat next to me, an echo,
you are both there & here

Poem for Emily

I awake at night, almost
perfect in my being, my
naked body dancing

against the dull kitchen
light, imagining how our
shadows would glow

together if we allowed
them to be, dancing
together, in pale light,

or if we ripped curtains
wide open, dancing,
the glare of moonlight

holding two bodies,
like love in a cup

A Dance (after Williams)

my mind & me, my own
Lake Texoma, a question
as to how or what we came

into being, this is a question,
each night among cigarettes
& confusion, how the dalliance

of the water top could bury
so much, I forgot as much
talking today, talking to you,

so sweet the gentle porch
in an odd July rain, we grow
differently, in different times,

the pear I gave you today,
bears the fruit I imagine

Buck's Pear Tree

you are not here, as cigarettes
from an open pack, dwindle,
each one a memory, we have

died and are dying for the lack
of nights alone, alone simply
for the occasion of smoke

& remembrance, of how
the once did & then does,
cigarette smoke longs

for the breath of memory,
of how we could've been
or how we couldn't

each puff lasting
on the body like memory

Memory, like a Cancer

I don't know, I don't know
where to turn, to work or love,
I have grown younger these days

abstraction is no longer
the vehicle of life,
of love, its own testament,

I want to return to the clouds,
of Constable, perhaps, to see
in them such surroundings

& to withdraw within them,
my own place, my own room,
a keyboard called my own,

where the banal exceeds
enunciation over denotation

Poem for Greg Reimen I

Van Gogh had his doubts,
his last painting, a road
leading to nowhere

as I do mine, most mornings,
like sunlight reflected
upon a coffee pot,

and my indifference,
each day becomes
a wheatfield, filled,

with the love of
impossibility, of the love,
one struggles for

before one surmounts
indifference, & goes to work

A Van Gogh Wheatfield

love is the laughter
in a conversation
when lofty ideas

express themselves,
meaninglessly, as if
one could or would ever

begin to understand,
the symbols, words or
brush strokes signify

art is the art of laughter,
however painful it appears,
yet it's not the artifact,

meaning as such can
only be performed

Poem for Greg Reimen II

and then after, how we
can clean up the stuff,
left over by laughter,

not just studios or desktops,
but concepts of why man
decided to walk upright,

in the first place, & where
he thought he was going,
leaving traces of existence,

what were they thinking,
& what are we thinking,
thinking about their thinking

until we laugh out loud,
nothing, or anything, is possible

Poem for Greg Reimen III

last night your hand held
so much of me, so much
of my life & time, I felt

this morning, I held
eternity in an hour, you
have given me so much,

in so little time, I have
time, to reflect so much upon
your face in streetlight

what light, the night allows,
& then we walked toward
the someplace, toward home,

the place of music & poetry,
the place inside the night

So much

I've wandered the streets
all night smelling the smell
only place has to offer,

when you left you took
a part of me, the part
Ahab knew was missing,

today, I limp badly, though
there is no good way to limp,
I have tried with my hands,

to hold the moments together,
but time has a way of making
us, disappear, into silence,

life is one cigarette after another,
filled with talking & smoke

And yet so little

fate sometimes deals us
a bad hand, like finding
one's self too old

in a very young world,
in which love evaporates
like dew on a July lawn,

even the books have become
rotting signatures of the possible,
I should have read *The Winter's*

Tale, a daughtered world
& a daughterless father
couldn't know the circumstance,

the grayness in the glass, tells me
as much, mornings I choose to awake

And yet less.

I can't begin to understand
the dynamics of love, words
fill the space between two people,

then fade as grasses turn brown,
turning the heavens, a cylindrical
shift in a broken clock, together,

we must have gotten something
wrong, but some things do
matter, a world doesn't rest

on ideas, we have our lives
to contend with, someone
somewhere must've known this,

I'll return to my work as you
will return, always in there

An Understanding

at four in the morning
I find you, crapped out,
longing my life away

listening to old songs
in a new found head,
driving my life away

realizing I can't begin
again, staring out darkened
windows, wishing for spring

again, knowing, falling
in love with love is like
falling into make believe,

wishing to get back, again,
wishing to get to Syracuse

A Boy from Syracuse

the exchange of subjectivities
is *Eros* in nature
as the desire to be an other

allows one to give one's self
to the other, to the body
and the blood of the other,

Americans, by nature, are too
Protestant in their denials,
the medievalist Adams knew this,

as did Emerson before him,
expressing the self as a raincoat,
not allowing the rain of other in,

Eros is more power than a loaded gun,
yet softer than an island rain

St. Maarten / St. Martin

because I do find love
so enticing, I've walked
across meadows, it's yellow

fields do find me sometimes
as the summer ends, as autumn
crisps the skies, we do not

always know the love seasons
bring home to us, how
the suddenness of the sky

walks beneath our feet
in the details of memory,
there was someone there

once, an understanding, or
a return, to the unexpected

I Need a Better Grip

morning rests on a coffee cup,
pale gray like September
pecans, heavy this year

we turn, & turn around,
hoping to get this right
this time, for once

the night has left reading
behind making the day
necessary, & desire

makes the small things
like breakfast, one's
ablutions, love, familiar

hope is one's self, naked,
dressing, to start the day

Hope

after the sun has fallen
but before it's done,
I lift myself up

& return to walking
to the place I am going
beyond here but not far

just past the place
of before, where sunlight
takes no shelter until

night absorbs its fall
where the find is already
forgotten, after twilight calls

the ones I've loved are with me,
though I leave them here

The Trudge

if you were a surgeon,
could I trust my knife
with your hands, knowing

how delicately I treasure
the things you cut away
to save, me from myself

I have a difficulty, not so
much in the saving, but
in cutting the me from me

if I were on your table,
beneath your light and assistants,
would the operation succeed

knowing grace works, & does
not work in mysterious ways

A Question

we have lived too long under
influence, lady liberty leading
the people, but that is too French

today, the Statue of Liberty,
another token of the French
is shut down, but will reopen

when the scare of writing
open words on a scant page
ceases to be a terror, these

poems have been sonnets
as I remember them to be
a condition of thought,

only to disturb a nation, over
I'm not, but I'm settling

Last Poem

Randy Prus, photo by Stan Alluisi

BIOS

Randy Prus is Professor of English and Humanities at Southeastern Oklahoma State University. He has published three chapbooks, *Ice, A New Time in a Very Old World,* and *Songs of the South and Slightly West.*

Ethan Prus creates comics and paintings in Southern Oklahoma. To see his artwork, visit *jelloween.com*

www.heartlink.com

Made in the USA
San Bernardino, CA
12 December 2015